My Heart is in the East

My Heart is in the East

Jessica Litwak

My Heart is in the East, Copyright © 2014 Jessica Litwak

All rights reserved.

CAUTION: Professionals and amateurs are hereby warned that *My Heart is in the East* is subject to a royalty. It is fully protected under the copyright laws of the United States of America, Dominion of Canada, United Kingdom, and all British Commonwealth countries, and all countries covered by the International Copyright Union, the Pan-American Copyright Convention, the Universal Copyright Convention, the Berne Convention, and of all countries with which the United States of America has reciprocal copyright relations. All rights, including professional/ amateur stage rights, motion picture, recitation, lecturing, public reading, radio broadcasting, television, video or sound taping, video or sound recording, all other forms of mechanical or electronic reproduction, such as CD-ROM, CD-I, DVD, information storage and retrieval systems and photocopying, and rights of translation into foreign languages, are strictly reserved. Particular emphasis is placed upon the matter of readings, permission for which must be secured from the Author's agent in writing. All inquiries concerning rights should be addressed to: Susan Schulman of Susan Schulman Literary Agency, 454 West 44th Street, New York, NY 10036, or emailed to Susan Schulman at susan@schulmanagency.com. No professional performance of the Play may be given without obtaining in advance the written permission of Susan Schulman Literary Agency, and paying the requisite fee

All rights are strictly reserved. No part of this book may be reproduced in any form or by any electronic or mechanical means, including information storage and retrieval systems, without permission in writing from the Author's agent, except by a reviewer, who may quote brief passages in a review. Any members of educational institutions wishing to photocopy part or all of the work for classroom use, or publishers who would like to obtain permission to include the work in an anthology, should send their inquires to: Susan Schulman of Susan Schulman Literary Agency, 454 West 44th Street, New York, NY 10036, or email Susan Schulman at susan@schulmanagency.com.

Special Notice:
Anyone receiving permission to produce *My Heart is in the East* is required to give credit to the Author as sole and exclusive Author of the Play on the title page of all programs distributed in connection with performances of the Play and in all instances in which the title of the Play appears for purposes of advertising, publicizing or otherwise exploiting the Play and/or production thereof. The name of the Author must appear on a separate line, on which no other name appears, immediately beneath the title and in size of type equal to 50% of the size of the largest, most prominent letter used for the title of the Play. No person, firm, or entity may receive credit larger or more prominent than that accorded the Author.

My heart is in the East
But the rest of me far in the West – Yehuda Halevi (1090)

> In darkness photographs and words appear in faster and faster succession with music as the recorded voices of 3 Men and 3 Women of different voices, ages, cultures and ethnicities overlap.

WOMEN	MEN
Peace	Peace

WOMEN

Is impossible.

WOMEN	MEN
War.	War.

MAN ONE

Reigns over my land.

WOMAN ONE

Death.

MAN TWO

Death.

WOMAN TWO

In abundance.

WOMEN	MEN
This is the way it is.	This is the way it is.
And the way it always was.	And the way it will always be.

JESSICA LITWAK

MAN THREE

You cannot.

WOMAN THREE

You will not.

MAN ONE

Ever.

WOMAN ONE

Abide,

MAN THREE

Fathom, or

WOMAN THREE

Delight

MAN ONE

Delight

WOMEN   MEN
In me   In me.

WOMAN ONE

You prostrate yourself on the floor.

MAN TWO

You fast every day for a month.

WOMAN TWO

You fast only one day a year.

MAN THREE

You pray sitting in chairs.

My Heart is in the East

WOMEN	MEN
You shroud your women.	You pimp your women.

WOMAN THREE
Your loud music and television wakes me at 3 a.m.

MAN ONE
Your call to prayer wakes me at 3:00 a.m.

WOMEN	MEN
You are heathen, uncivilized.	You are heathen, uncivilized.

WOMAN ONE
You cannot.

WOMEN	MEN
You will not, now or ever	You will not now, not ever

WOMAN TWO
Feed my children.

MAN TWO
Save my people.

WOMAN THREE
You cannot. Will not.

WOMEN	MEN
Hold. Care. Rescue.	Hold. Care. Rescue.

MAN THREE
Provide safe passage.

WOMAN ONE
You will always

MEN	WOMEN
Judge. Hate. Spy on.	Judge. Hate. Spy on.

MAN ONE

You will always

WOMEN	MEN
Be suspicious of	Be suspicious of

WOMAN TWO

Fear.

MAN TWO

My Strange

WOMAN THREE

Name.

MAN THREE

Clothes.

WOMAN ONE

Food.

MAN ONE

Smell.

WOMEN	MEN
You Al Jezeera fundamentalist barbarian.	You Fox News judgmental racist capitalist.
You backwoods, back road, back door, ignorant luddite.	You rich, soft handed privileged fascist neophyte.
You primordial peasant.	You pale faced killer.

MAN TWO
You lock up the Black and the Brown.

WOMAN TWO
Your terrorism undermines our precious liberty and our pursuit of happiness.

MAN THREE
You plot against us.

MEN	WOMEN
You steal our jobs.	You shoot us.
You sneak up on us.	You annex, appropriate,
You take us down.	occupy and slaughter us.

WOMAN THREE
You sneak up on us. You take us down.

MEN	WOMEN
You annex, appropriate, occupy and slaughter us.	You eviscerate us. You register us.

MAN ONE
You detain and deport us.

WOMAN ONE
You make us invisible.

MEN	WOMEN
You fly planes into our monuments.	You make us defensive.

MAN TWO
You destroy our traditions.

WOMAN TWO
You vilify our sanctuaries.

MEN	WOMEN
You murder us.	You murder us.

A beat of silence. Lights fade up slowly on Miri and Ishmael. He is on one side of the stage digging a grave. She is on the other sitting in a pile of bunched up papers trying to write. A phone rings. Ishmael answers his phone. A paper airplane flies in and hits her.

MIRI
Iraq.

ISHMAEL
America?

Lights shift.

MIRI
Akram Rusafi, an Iraqi professor wants me to attend an Arts Festival in Basra, to teach workshops in puppet building. He says he's heard about the Jewish History scholar in New York who makes puppets with brains. *"Puppets that inspire debate without inciting fury."* The visa has to be quickly arranged. I must decide by the end of the day. Akram pleads: *"So few Westerners will travel to Iraq these days. Miri will you come?"* Should I / go?

ISHMAEL

Akram, wants me to translate for some American woman teaching puppets. PUPPETS? My country is under siege, children in refugee camps, power goes out every 15 minutes, no one has enough to eat and they spend money for a Western lady to teach – what? How to make a fucking puppet? Akram seduces: *"Your English is a gift that will propel you to the West"* I don't want to be propelled to the WEST! *"You have been digging graves for shit pay, Ishmael. A job that shames your family. Put your politics aside – be a man."* / America?

MIRI

Iraq?

MIRI AND ISHMAEL

I am advised against it.

MIRI	ISHMAEL (SINGING)
"The Department of State warns U.S. Citizens against all travel to Iraq! Travel within Iraq remains DANGEROUS."	*"Kill those fucking Yankees who have been torturing Iraqi captives / Kill those fucking Yankees-"*

MIRI

But I remember a desperate protest long ago the night before that President gave the order to bomb Baghdad. On the streets waving signs at traffic – hoping to bring some last minute sense to the power machine in Washington, cars honking, patriots spitting. At 5:30 am Iraqi time the bombs begin to fall. We watch them exploding on television – small bursts of green light.

Lights shift. They both walk.

ISHMAEL	MIRI
I go to the fields.	
	I go east. Across Central Park to the East Side.
Where my guys are. You can't really call it a field it's just a pile of dirt with a half built bridge in the middle – my guys are kicking a deflated foot ball into the dust.	
	Metropolitan Museum of Art. Second floor, third hallway. The Islamic Wing.
I don't tell them about the job offer. I am ashamed that I even speak English as good as I do.	
	I stand in the doorway of an ancient room, which is a replica of a room in Medieval Spain. The Golden Age. La Convivencia. The Co-existence. When poetry made peace possible between Muslims and Jews.
None of these guys have work. If they could speak English would they take this job? No. They hate America. These guys are my sanctuary.	This history is my sanctuary.

As Ishmael kicks a deflated soccer ball against a wall, lights come up on a museum exhibit: A room in Ancient Cordoba. Miri reaches out to touch the exhibit. An alarm goes off. She yanks her hand back.

My Heart is in the East

ISHMAEL	MIRI
I am not really there in that field with the guys. I am writing poems in my head. If they knew I was rhyming they'd punch me. They want me to stay present. In their world. Not off in Rhymeland. I keep my poems inside me. Hidden.	In this ancient room calligraphy lines the walls:
	soft letters in gold. The voices of the ancient poets inscribed on every surface. I can hear them. They speak in Arabic and Hebrew and just for me in Modern
Another sin: I write my poems in English.	English a language not yet born.
	I have found this fragment of an ancient poem.

MIRI

Which leads me to my favorite part of the exhibit. There is a wax model of an ancient Arab man, pen in hand – a poet? A serving woman watches him – A Jew? They are in a room in Cordoba, Spain. One thousand years ago. I have tried to write their story-

> She reaches into the exhibit.
> Alarm. She pulls her hand away.

ISHMAEL

Each time I kick the ball I am telling a lie. Each time I write a poem I am kicking my country in the eye, screaming at the sky, hearing my mother cry.

MIRI

I come to this exhibit two three times a week now. The President has threatened the closing of the Islamic Wing. New rules about Homeland Security.

> She leans towards the exhibit.
> Alarm.

ISHMAEL	**MIRI**
I am writing a secret book of secret poems.	I am writing a book about the Convivencia.

MIRI

Trying to write.

ISHMAEL

What good is poetry? Unless I use it as a sword.

ISHMAEL	**MIRI**
	I will go to Iraq.
I will take this job.	
	See the truth of the world.
I'll fuck with her American mind.	
I'll do it in English.	
I'll do it in Rhyme.	

> A paper airplane flies in and hits Ishmael. He puts it in his pocket. Lights shift. The Basra airport.

MIRI

Basra airport. Two bodyguards in shiny suits. They look more Italian Mafioso than Arab soldier. I see the bulges of guns in their pockets. I meet Akram, my Iraqi host. He is beautiful, deep eyes, strong arms. In urgent whispers he warns me to conceal my citizenship by not speaking English in public. The risk of kidnapping is high, and my kidnapping would be for him, extremely inconvenient. I will be 100% dependent on my translator. Who is my translator?

> Ishmael enters with a shovel and a shotgun over his shoulder.

ISHMAEL
Call me Ishmael.

MIRI
What?

ISHMAEL
Moby Dick. Sick. Don't fail. To see. The irony.

MIRI
I am Miri.

ISHMAEL
Mariam. My Grandmother's name, the same.

MIRI
Why the shovel and the shot gun?

ISHMAEL
For fun.

MIRI
Excuse me?

ISHMAEL
The jobs I do. A man these days needs more than two. Boneyards make my country's bed. Combat tends to turn us dead.

MIRI
You are a grave digger?

ISHMAEL
Hard times sister. Corpses rot and make us sick. Gotta get them down there quick. Good pay: by the body, not the day.

MIRI
Where do you bury the – ?

> He points to her feet. She looks down. She jumps. He laughs.

MIRI
Akram says: "Ishmael will be with you every day." You sure? I mean – HIM? *He'll* translate?

ISHMAEL
Tha's my fate. The English I jazz you with spins off my tongue.
Your life in my hands for the Arabic sung You won't understand, won't get the meaning, Of questions, commands, whispers or screaming.
You'll cling to my ear: "what did that man say?"
Your desperate confusion will just make my day.
You gonna see Iraq through my eyes.
No media lies. Justice, Mrs. America, is the meat of my thrust. Now pick up your bags and surrender your trust.

MIRI
Akram laughs: "*Ishmael is such a trickster.*" Akram tells me to get in the car. I get in the car. Akram on one side Ishmael on the other. The bodyguards in the front seat. We travel in the bulletproof vehicle to my hotel. Akram motions for me to cover myself. Ishmael keeps talking.

ISHMAEL

MY LAND
Was the garden of Eden.
Fertile crescent of the world.
One of the seven pearls.
MY LAND
Has a glorious past
For the last 8,000 years
Until your nation
Wracked our civilization
With occupation.
Raided our country, counted your spoils
And floated to victory on a wave of oil.
Who needs Eden when you got Exxon?
Who needs fertility – fruit, trees, grass
When you got fields and fields of fucking gas?

MIRI

"This is a bad checkpoint," Akram says, "cover your head, look down". I don't know what is "bad" about this particular checkpoint. None of them seem "good" to me. The gunman gestures at me through the window. I want to tell him I am only here to make puppets out of newspaper. He takes my passport and walks away. My bodyguard pulls out his gun and follows. I wonder if I will ever make it back to New York.
Then the bodyguard is running back towards to car "Yallah, Yallah!" The driver hits the accelerator, the bodyguard jumps into the moving car and we speed off to the next checkpoint.
Hopefully it's not a "bad" one.

ISHMAEL

The Dead.
Shed
Some respect, Man

Jessica Litwak

MIRI	ISHMAEL
	The Sacred is damned
Every few blocks the car stops, the driver turns on the inside light.	This war is a scam.
And a man with a rifle or	Waste of life.
a pistol or a machine gun,	Strife Makes everything grey.
sometimes wearing a mask,	No day Is spared the dread dark dance of death.
leans into the car,	
	The mess.
asks for identification, the	Of lead.
driver shows his ID, mumbles	And leather.
a nervous salutation, and	Of stormy weather. Look!
we are waved through.	
	He bled out:
The Roads are filled with	
tanks and lined with bill-	His heart scooped from his chest.
boards with photographs of	The rest Of him is over there.
martyrs and wanted men.	Some hair.
	A shoe.
Akram says that when the wanted	A blue Piece of shirt.
men are caught and killed	And over there is another
their pictures are crossed off	who has come to harm
with a black spray painted X.	He's missing an arm
No one knows who is in charge,	Two sons. Equal. Dead.
who is manning the checkpoints:	
police or rebels, Shia, or Sunni,	This war is a sore Edge.
rageful or indifferent.	
There are so many guns in Iraq	Between this world and
that they begin to look like toys.	the other one.

ISHMAEL

The better one,
The nether one,
The shit show,
The limbo,
The up
the down,
the in
the out,
The over. They tell me "get them in the ground by sundown.
Cover them with stone.
No coffins from here are going home."
No tears, no poems, no love, no lust,
Just ashes to ashes and dust to dust.

MIRI

Dust is everywhere, on the streets of Basra. Dust that blows in from the desert, dust from the perpetual construction that will never be finished, the city is filled with half built bridges, bridges leading nowhere.

ISHMAEL

Two sides
To every gory
Story

MIRI	ISHMAEL
Akram wants me to conceal my female curves with my shawl and my hair with a head scarf.	Two sides To glory Two sides To war Two sides. Tonight along my street, Two more bodies-new dead meat Two lives. One from each Two boys side. about the same age Two small reports on a newspaper page They weren't brothers. They shot each other. BOOM. Fell in the line. At the same time. Now these two are ready for worms But I don't squirm. Ain't no souls I gotta save.
He cautions me most of all always and without question	
	I'm just in the business of digging graves.
To hide the fact that I am Jewish.	

ISHMAEL

Wait. Akram! She's Jewish?

Lights shift.

MIRI

I go to the water fountain in the hotel hallway after Akram and Ishmael leave me for the night. A man appears. He grabs me and shoves me into the wall. I think he works for the hotel. I think he's the man that brought up my suitcase. He clutches my neck. Stops my breath. He leans his mouth to my ear and whispers one word: "America"

Lights shift.

MIRI
In the morning Ishmael is hanging out with the bodyguards, laughing. When he sees me he begins rhyming in English.

ISHMAEL
Death will come, no time to think, Need one last girl and one last drink.
When you're done with her, tell her: "Depart!" Cover your ears to her breaking heart.
As she protests, with fervent crying, Say: "Love you, Baby!" She knows you're lying.

MIRI
Do you really feel that way about women or are you being offensive for my benefit?

ISHMAEL
"Offensive" says the representative Of the free world of MORE And who would you be speaking for?
Not us, the IDP. Garden variety refugees.
The unhoused 850 thousand.
Conflict led us north on a hopeless course.
To Damp camps. Children and tanks. Some lived. Thanks.
My family ran to Syria to escape America.
Then ran back to our native land to elude the guns in Syrian hands.
My house hit twice. By Isis.
There are 13 of us in there now. Seeking cover-

MIRI
At least you can protect each other.

ISHMAEL
We try to supply. Assistance. But there is some resistance. A dead man cannot carry a dead man.

MIRI

Are you in danger here?

ISHMAEL

Are you a stranger here? Don't you cruise the news?
Don't you grasp the fast reality of doom as bombs go BOOM?
Every day of blood and mirth could be my last on planet earth.
Tomorrow it's me in a 6 foot ditch, that's life on Iraqi soil, bitch.

MIRI

Where is Akram?

ISHMAEL

Prince Charming say he has to go away – all day today.
You're ass is with me – Gonna translate your shit at university.

> Lights shift. They move. The university. Miri builds a puppet out of newspaper and tape as she addresses her class.

MIRI

OK. The first thing we did is make the puppet's brain. We put a secret or a memory or a wish inside and it became the brain. NOW Newspaper and masking tape form the head around it – a face emerges, and the stories come. Now please tell the stories of your puppets. (To Ishmael) Are you translating this?

ISHMAEL (IN ARABIC)

The first thing we did is make the puppet's brain. We put a secret or a memory or a wish inside and it became the brain.
NOW Newspaper and masking tape form the head around it – a face emerges, and the stories come. Tell the stories of the puppets.

MIRI

What did you tell them?

ISHMAEL
"Make what the white lady makes. Shove the paper into a face."

MIRI
Why is there just one girl and 17 boys?

ISHMAEL
Think hard Jewish Mama! Why are Muslim girls banned from Puppet Drama?

MIRI
The girl speaking. What is she/-

ISHMAEL
She is telling the story of when her brother beat her for flirting with a boy. I think her puppet is her.

MIRI
Translate her exact words.

ISHMAEL
"My virginity is like glass, if it breaks it is not my honor that is ruined, it is me."

MIRI
"My virginity is like glass"

ISHMAEL (IN ARABIC)
"My virginity is like glass"

MIRI
Oh my God. What's that boy doing?

ISHMAEL (IN ARABIC)
Stop it!

MIRI
He's thrashing her puppet! What's he shouting?

ISHMAEL (IN ARABIC)
You are a whore!

MIRI
WHAT?

ISHMAEL
You are a whore!

MIRI
She fell. Get up, off the floor, Honey. Help her.

ISHMAEL
She doesn't want me touching her. She says the destruction of the puppet was part of her play.

MIRI
Oh. Can we all imagine a different ending where the girl doesn't get hurt? Tell them.

ISHMAEL (IN ARABIC)
Think of a different ending.

MIRI
They are all talking at once.

ISHMAEL
The boys have ideas.

MIRI
What are they saying?

> She points to each student as Ishmael translates.

ISHMAEL

"She should kick him."
"She should run away and hide."
"She should do what he says."
"She should kill him."
"She should pray to Allah to help her."
"She should – "

MIRI

The girl! What did she say?

ISHMAEL

She said "The woman should kiss the man on the forehead and her forgiveness will make him ashamed of himself."

MIRI

Love trumps rage!

ISHMAEL

"Love trumps rage?"

MIRI

Yes.

ISHMAEL

Nothing trumps rage, Baby. Specially not love.

> Ishmael responds to a kid in the class.

ISHMAEL (IN ARABIC)

What?

MIRI
What?

ISHMAEL
That kid has something to say. Go on Mrs. America, make his day.

MIRI
What's he – ?

ISHMAEL
He's saying he was a prisoner of war but he can't remember the cell where he lived for 18 months. It bothers him.

MIRI
Does he remember anything at all?

ISHMAEL
He says "One Thing, An insect. A black beetle."

MIRI
His puppet looks like a beetle.

ISHMAEL
He says "I trapped him under a cup and kept him there to be my friend. I talked to him for nearly a week before he died. I even shared crumbs from my bread with him. But he didn't make it. I've never told anyone this. I … Named him … Ali."

MIRI
Let's try something. You want to try something? Ask him if he'll try something.

ISHMAEL (IN ARABIC)
You want to try something?

MIRI
Imagine you are the black beetle. Ali. Now try to see the cell through the bug's eyes. Look how he moves down the corridor of his imagination using his puppet to speak in the bug's voice. What's he saying?

ISHMAEL
"I see a crack in the wall… Bars on the window. Grey mattress, hole in the floor, the man: my friend. Oh God…"

MIRI
Is he OK?

ISHMAEL (IN ARABIC)
Are you OK?

ISHMAEL
Yes. He says "It's better to see."

MIRI
Tell him he's brave.

> Ishmael jumps up.

ISHMAEL
The guard says we have to split. Yallah, yallah! pack up your shit.

MIRI
What's going on?

ISHMAEL
We have to get you back to the hotel.

> They move fast. Back in the hotel lobby. She is still holding the puppet she was making.

MIRI

What is happening?

ISHMAEL

Bodyguard saw guns coming in through the back.
Just another afternoon in Basra, Iraq.

MIRI

There were guns at the school?

ISHMAEL

Relax, Mrs. American Jew.
Running from guns ain't nothing new.

> Ishmael takes the puppet from her and makes it talk.

ISHMAEL(AS PUPPET)

These people will murder you in your sleep.

MIRI

You have no heart.

ISHMAEL(AS PUPPET)

You made me. If there's no heart it's your fault.

MIRI

I can change that.

ISHMAEL(AS PUPPET)

Too late, I already have a brain.

MIRI

I'll make another puppet.

ISHMAEL (AS PUPPET)

You are marginalizing me!

MIRI

Marginalizing you? I wrote you.

ISHMAEL (AS PUPPET)

What gave you the right to write me?

> She takes the puppet away from him. She finishes making it.

ISHMAEL

Don't think you're gonna get an American hug, But I liked what you did with that boy and his bug.

MIRI

When will Akram be back?

ISHMAEL

What are you doing in Iraq?

MIRI

I am here to teach.

ISHMAEL

Not to preach? Tame the beast?
Those savage barbarians in the cruel Middle East?

MIRI
All I seem to be able to do with any success is make puppets out of newspaper. They make people feel free –

ISHMAEL
Are <u>you</u> free from desire, are you selfless and brave?
Or are you hunting for sainthood before hitting the grave?

MIRI
I want to have the courage/ to try-

ISHMAEL
Courage? Generosity? The Call from above? Are you reaching for peace – Or are you looking for love?

MIRI
Love? No!

ISHMAEL
Then what, Yo?

MIRI
Poetry.

ISHMAEL
Poetry?

MIRI
I am writing a book.

ISHMAEL
You write white woman? You working on some drafts? I thought your thing was arts and crafts?

MIRI
Writing can be lonely. My apartment is filled with puppets.

ISHMAEL
So you penning a study about your paper head buddies?

MIRI
My book is about Medieval Spain: La Convivencia. The coexistence.

ISHMAEL
Yo Puppet Lady from afar, I ain't asked you for no seminar.

MIRI
It was a beautiful golden age when our peoples – yours and mine – were united by poetry. These huge poetry contests were held in Hebrew and Arabic – a dynamic exchange between Muslims and Jews.

ISHMAEL
What?

MIRI
It's true. They found these poems in the Cairo Genizah, a holy graveyard for Jewish texts. There was this one paper. Fragment T-S 143.46. It was half of a poem by Dunash bin Labrat, the first Jewish poet to incorporate Arabic rhythms into his poems.

ISHMAEL
He did what?

MIRI
Jews were inspired by the complex forms of Arabic poetry.

ISHMAEL
Go on.

MIRI
So the scholars assumed this fragment was a farewell poem to his wife. But then they uncovered fragment T-S 144.47 – the other half of the letter. This one was signed! The poem was not written by Dunash to his wife! It was written by his wife to him. It was the single example of a Jewish woman's poetry in the entire Genizah. That's what my book is about.

He is listening.

MIRI
Intriguing, right?

He snaps out of it.

ISHMAEL
What use is moldy historical dirt, to the current hell of life on earth?

MIRI
In Cordoba peace between our peoples was real and that/ means we-

ISHMAEL
Idealism! The schism between your world and mine – you want peace and love to shine? That's insulting to my existence-wake up North American Princess-

MIRI
Why are you always rapping?

ISHMAEL
"Rapping?" Tha's what be happ'ning?

MIRI

You got that from us.

ISHMAEL

You sussed! Comprehend the one friend coming outta your corrupt nation – Hip Hop, Dawg-ette.

MIRI

Can't you just talk normally?

ISHMAEL

Like what? Like you write? Normally? How do you write? What do you write? what what what what what what / what?

MIRI

I haven't been able to write anything in weeks.

ISHMAEL

Oh shit. Might as well be you under this rock. Ain't nothing so cut-throat as writer's block.

MIRI

I am sure you've never had it.

ISHMAEL

Self doubt. The privileged pearl of the American girl.

MIRI

What?

ISHMAEL

So, since you can't create, this trip to Iraq is your big escape.

MIRI

I am here as a bridge to peace. I'M A BRIDGE.

ISHMAEL

Look around you, Girl, your eyes be crusted, All the bridges around here are busted.

MIRI

I am trying to do some good!

ISHMAEL

Do good do gooder western lady syn drome sin drone dropping your liberal intentions with infinitesimal dimensions on our heads – but we're still dead – This ain't no safari Baby – This shit is real life, this shit /is –

MIRI

I AM SORRY FOR WHAT MY COUNTRY DID TO YOUR COUNTRY.

>She throws the puppet. They look at each other.
>Lights shift.
>Ishmael speaks to the audience.

ISHMAEL

We are at a restaurant. She is the only Westerner. A guy comes in. I recognize him. He is not one of us. He is trouble – if he is here that means more of them are coming. The haters. The Decapitators. If I point her out that would be the end of her. I don't. I go over to Akram and whisper in his ear. He gestures like a prince and everyone rises. He speaks urgently, quietly: *To the boat!*

MIRI

We are on a boat. At the junction of two rivers.

ISHMAEL

Where the Tigris meets the Euphrates.

MIRI

We are on the top deck where two young theatre companies and have gathered to take in the view: Saddam's abandoned yacht and palace, the submerged wrecks along the river, the desert. The Egyptian company of actors begins dancing and chanting regional folk songs. They are rowdy and proud, waving the Egyptian flag up and down to the music. They bring the women into the center – we are a rebellion. We jump and sway, we rock the boat.
Suddenly, on the other end of the deck a group of Iraqi actors began their own chants and dances. A call and response between the two countries emerges. "IRAQ!" "EGYPT!" "EGYPT!" "IRAQ!".

Ishmael makes the loud noise of a police siren.

MIRI

A police boat is following us. The music must have alerted the militia. But Akram says the police boat is there because there is one American on board. Me.
All I can do is dance. An elderly Egyptian professor calls to me over the music: "This is the only way we will unite the world – with art!" Akram is dancing near me, but we are not touching.. He's so young and so handsome. He moves me. His dark eyes. His hard life. I wonder if he's flirting with / me-

Lights shift.

ISHMAEL

Mrs. America. Let me translate something for you. Straight up. No rhyme. Akram is saying he wants you to sneak a bottle of wine into your hotel room –

MIRI

I know what he is saying. He is speaking English.

ISHMAEL
He is saying other shit in Arabic to his friends.

MIRI
Like what?

ISHMAEL
You know what.

MIRI
Really?

ISHMAEL
Have some respect for yourself, Lady. Wrestle with your book. Not with Akram.

MIRI
Akram and I are going to write the book together. He's interested in the ancient interaction between / our peoples.

ISHMAEL
He's interested in your ass. I see what's going on Baby.

MIRI
Nothing is going on. He's 20 years younger than me!

ISHMAEL
Lust beats math.

She turns to the audience.

MIRI
Akram and I do smuggle wine into my hotel room. I don't know if I should tell this part-

ISHMAEL
It's about sex.

MIRI
No, it's / not-

ISHMAEL
In a war zone / 6,000 miles from her home

MIRI
6,000 miles from her home/ in semi darkness

ISHMAEL
In a hotel room secured by armed guards, at the center of a storm of international fury/ as the oil fields burn,

MIRI
As the oil fields burn, and the sky is brown with dust, and the voices of protest are locked away / and the artists are fighting for resurgence

ISHMAEL
And the artists are fighting for resurgence, as the censored news blares a limited freedom of information, as injustice persists, and pride/and suspicion

MIRI
And suspicion. As huge amounts of cash slip from palm to palm, as children throw stones at stray cats by a river of garbage, as the bright eyes of the women shine over covered faces, and men hug each other, and people laugh / as ancient tensions are re-kindled,

ISHMAEL
As ancient tensions are re-kindled, and a world away a president is elected, and bombs go off in the north / and the globe reels

MIRI

And the globe reels from post traumatic stress that stretches back past Isis, past Al Qaeda, past the towers, past Mohammed all the way to the first exploding atom that birthed the cells of human war/ Here in this tiny place,

ISHMAEL

Here in this tiny place,
as all that swirls around her,
in the middle of/ everything and nothing,

MIRI

Everything and nothing
in this invisible,
replicated, yet never before seen room
that could be Verona, or Hades, or Hiroshima,/
the woman relents

ISHMAEL

the woman relents.
And allows the man to reach up and stroke her hair.

MIRI

She watches as he unbuttons the white shell buttons on her polka dot blouse.
Wow, he says.
He has seen people shot right in front of him.
Now he sees her.
His fingers burn her skin.
She takes his thick black hair in her fists, and kisses him with the weight of both their civilizations, the way women have kissed men for centuries, the way no woman has kissed before.
She kisses him beyond age and beyond culture, her story so far from his own.

He whispers – This is the only way we will unite the world-with sex!
She knows nothing can happen for them in time or space outside of this hotel room.
Hands cannot be held in cafes or movie theatres, families cannot be met or birthdays celebrated.
But in this bed, full of blood and fire she feels Alive.
He will shower and return to the world and the God and the women and the path that is allowed him.
She will gather herself and fly back to the free world and take up where she left off.
And no one, not even the hotel staff cleaning up the illegal wine bottle and the soiled sheets will ever imagine what has occurred between them.
Like the uncertainty principle only the observers will be able to prove its existence.
But it flowers in her, she pledges to devote her work and life to the enrichment and salvation of his country.
His country that was ravaged by hers.
Like she was ravaged here tonight, willingly, by him.
This sex is not faceless, or nameless.
It is political and religious and important.
It will shift in some small unseen way, the fabric of international peace.
It is Resonant, and
Shattering,
And Brave.

>Ishmael claps slowly. She glares at him. Lights shift.

ISHMAEL

Things are getting worse by the hour. Guys are missing from the field. Kasim has joined up with the killers, Ibrahim is found missing his head. She is getting ready to leave. This job is almost over. The door of servitude is closing. But so is the window.

Miri packs up her puppet and gets ready to leave.

MIRI

There are 9 checkpoints on the way to the airport. At 4 of them I receive a full body search. At one checkpoint 5 miles from the airport I say goodbye to my body guards. I look at Akram. I try not to turn bright red. We have a plan to meet in Beirut to work on our book. I say Goodbye to Akram.

ISHMAEL

You say Goodbye to Ishmael.

MIRI

Goodbye, Ishmael.

He leans in and whispers.

ISHMAEL

Get me out of Iraq.

MIRI

What? What? Suddenly I am pushed into the final airport transport – Yallah! Yallah! we drive off they disappear in the dust. What did he say?

A paper airplane flies in. He picks it up.

ISHMAEL

She leaves, I am set free. I go to Akram for the translation fee. I grovel. Forty dollars for my trouble.

MIRI

In the Dubai airport, I take off my head scarf, buy a glass of champagne and drink it out in the open. The more I drink the wiser I become. I devise solutions for all the problems-war-peace, man-woman, East – West, America-Iraq. When I board the plane I have a list of resolutions to pass on to the State Department. By the time I land at JFK, I have forgotten what they were.

ISHMAEL

The shadow comes over my house.
Things turn south.
I am digging graves full time.
Alone in silence with my rhyme.

MIRI

In the taxi cab from JFK my heart is still in the East – I must be crying because the taxi driver offers me a tissue. "Shukran", I say. He smiles. An Arab immigrant, he thinks I am being friendly. Actually, I just forgot where I was.
Ishmael is digging.

ISHMAEL

I hear every sound, every word, every ghost,
The youngest voices haunt me the most.
The one that dies crying alone in the night.
The one that dies telling lies to his wife

MIRI

I go to the museum every day now. The Islamic Wing has begun to be dismantled. I have to climb over boxes to get to my room. The woman is gone, and one of the man's hands is missing – the one that was holding the pen.

> She leans into the exhibit.
> Nothing happens.

ISHMAEL

I hear every hope dripping on, every loss The souls leaking out as their limbs gather moss.

MIRI

I work hard to get the funding and the Visa for Beirut. It is more difficult to get the Middle East now – everything is changing. More deportations. People held for hours at the airports.

ISHMAEL

I hear all these guys in their new dirt bed
As I'll hear each of you, my dear future dead.

> Lights out on Ishmael.

MIRI

Things have gotten strained with Akram over Skype. I nag him about turning in pages for our book. He wants to dictate his stories and have me type. We argue over sentences. Culture. Gender. Age. Whatever the reason. We do not completely understand each other. But still, I-

> Phone rings. Miri picks up her phone. Lights up on Ishmael holding his phone. Staring at it. Unable to dial.

MIRI (INTO THE PHONE)

Hello? Akram! How are / you?

ISHMAEL

When your will is broken you need to call someone.

MIRI (INTO THE PHONE)

Did you get my message about the funding for / Beirut?

ISHMAEL

But you can't bring yourself / to make the call.

MIRI

The money came through. And your visa. I am so excited – / What?

ISHMAEL

You buy the minutes. You charge the phone. / You dial.

MIRI (INTO THE PHONE)

So what, you're not / coming?

ISHMAEL

Let it ring. / And then

MIRI (INTO THE PHONE)

Not now or not / ever?

ISHMAEL

And then you/ just-

MIRI

Marginalized?/ I didn't mean-

ISHMAEL

And then you hang up.

MIRI

Akram? Hello?

> Miri hangs up. Ishmael makes the call. Her phone rings. She answers.

MIRI

Akram?

ISHMAEL
Ishmael.

MIRI
Ishmael?

ISHMAEL
From Iraq.

MIRI
Oh. Yes. Sorry. How are you?

ISHMAEL
My brother joined ISIS. My father hides under the bed. I don't know how much longer I will be alive. Oh Sorry. "Fine. How are you?"

MIRI
You broke your-

ISHMAEL
Rhyme. Yeah. Somebody shot it. You writing your book?

MIRI
What gives me the right to write? I am still / blocked-

ISHMAEL
We all got problems. / I was-

MIRI
I was just speaking to Akram / he-

ISHMAEL
I need your help.

MIRI

Oh. / OK.

ISHMAEL

They are going to kill me.

MIRI

What? / Who?

ISHMAEL

My brother found out that I am on a list. They've been watching me. I speak English. Translate for Westerners. / I don't know how long-

MIRI

I don't know how I can help / you.

ISHMAEL

I need to get out of Iraq. Fast. This is not easy for me. I hate to have to fucking ask / you-

MIRI

Wait. I can't get you into the U.S. / But-

ISHMAEL

I'm not begging for – What? But what?

MIRI

There's well, Beirut.

ISHMAEL

Beirut?

MIRI

The visa won't be a problem for you / But you-

ISHMAEL

Would you meet me / there?

MIRI

I could. I have some funding. It was for Akram and me. I can buy the plane tickets. I already have mine. But I can't help you much after that you'll be,/ you'll be-

ISHMAEL

I'll be. I'll be. I'll be a refugee.

MIRI

Yes.

ISHMAEL

It's very IN these days. Anyone who is anyone is a refugee.

MIRI

You still have a sense of humor.

ISHMAEL

Only on Tuesdays.

MIRI

OK.

> Lights shift. A paper airplane flies in. Miri catches it.

MIRI

On the plane I drink several glasses of Chardonnay. An Egyptian woman is sitting next to me. "I have cancer" I pretend not to hear her. "My mother died of cancer." I stare out the window. "The week my mother died the uprising exploded around us. I could not get out of bed for my grief. But one morning I went down to Tahir Square. The revolution saved my life. We have a saying in my country: when the mother dies, the motherland takes over." That's a good saying. "I am not afraid to die" You're brave. "I'm Egyptian, Madame. What's your superpower?" For the rest of the flight I think: I wish I had a motherland. I wish I had a superpower.

> Lights shift.

ISHMAEL
I snuck out in the middle of the night.

MIRI
I am glad you got here safely.

ISHMAEL
Now what?

MIRI
I don't know. This was supposed to be a trip for Akram and me. I have some historical research contacts. I have a room in a hotel.

> He walks.

MIRI
That's the wrong/ way-

ISHMAEL
Yallah, Yallah!

> She follows

MIRI
Can you slow down?

ISHMAEL
Is something wrong with you?

MIRI
No.

ISHMAEL
Then be quiet and walk. Here.

> He stops. She stops.

MIRI
A liquor store?

ISHMAEL
Buy vodka.

MIRI
I thought Muslims don't drink.

ISHMAEL
I am free to drink in Beirut! You are not my boss!

MIRI
Why are you acting this way?

ISHMAEL
You think because you paid my way you own me?

MIRI
We can get vodka at the hotel.

She walks away.

ISHMAEL

Akram's moving to Canada.

She stops.

ISHMAEL

He got a Work Visa. A job at a University. A new girlfriend. He didn't tell you.

She walks again. He follows.

ISHMAEL

An Iraqi lady in Vancouver.

MIRI

I kept saying the wrong things. Marginalizing him without meaning to. A colleague sent me an article called "How To Talk To Arab Men." But / I-

ISHMAEL

"*How To Talk To Arab Men?*"

MIRI

I know. Here.

She stops.

ISHMAEL

We both stay here at this hotel?

She walks. Stops again.

MIRI

Here.

ISHMAEL

In one room?

MIRI

For now. It's all I have.

ISHMAEL

There is only one bed.

MIRI

Akram was the first person I had been with in a very long time. It's not as though I am in the habit/ of –

ISHMAEL

Being a whore?

MIRI

You are a misogynist jerk!

ISHMAEL

The traditional accusation from the North American Female: *"You Woman hater"*!

MIRI

You people do hate women.

MIRI	ISHMAEL
You want women covered up and silent, walking two feet behind you.	We adore women. We treat them better than your men treat yours and they are faithful/ to us-

MIRI
Saddam Hussein hung a woman from one leg during her period so her menstrual blood would drown her.

ISHMAEL
In Abu Ghrahib the soldiers humiliated religious men by making them masturbate in front of female officers.

MIRI	ISHMAEL
You think I'm like them? All Americans are whores and pigs? That's the terrorist propaganda.	You think all Muslims are terrorists? That's Western propaganda

MIRI
You are so ignorant!

ISHMAEL
You want Mr. Ignorant to pay you back for the ticket?

MIRI
What?

ISHMAEL
Give you sex?

He grabs her, kisses her neck.

ISHMAEL
Do you like this?

MIRI
No.

ISHMAEL
Want me to do it to you like Akram?

                          MIRI

STOP IT

                         ISHMAEL

DO I DISGUST YOU?

                    She pushes him away.

                          MIRI

I AM NOT YOUR FUCKING ENEMY.

                    He huddles in a corner, ashamed. He takes a
                    small photo out of his pocket. He hands it to her.

                         ISHMAEL

Mama and me. Hot tea.
Late September rain trying to kill snails with my train.
She chides "Careful child not so wild –
That train is not a tank a tank is not an answer.
Go peaceful boy – don't commit murder with your toy
Lead us to a better time,
Do your rhymes – Turn the clock
Back to sacred days of old Iraq."

                          MIRI

Is your Mother-?

                         ISHMAEL

These are the things I remember:
Her eyes turning red at the list of dead
Every day an uncle or cousin or friend
Seemed to meet his bloody end.
"Don't go to war Son" she'd say every day
"don't fight, write
your own world. Kiss girls."

He hoists his arm up like a gun.

ISHMAEL
Mama BOOM Mama BOOM Mama BOOM Maaaammmaaa! These are the things I remember: The police came.
Night made the sky the color of her hair.
She was never not ever not never coming home.
Bullet through the evening mist.
Had to add Mama to the list.
She was my sun.

He cries. She sits beside him.

MIRI
My mother jumped off a bridge.

ISHMAEL
What?

MIRI
Mississippi River. Privileged pearl of self doubt.

ISHMAEL
Sorry.

MIRI
I don't remember much about her. Except some parts of the songs she sang.

Pause. He begins to sing.

ISHMAEL (SINGING)
Yalla tnam Rima, yalla yijeeha elnoum

Miri sings too.

MIRI (SINGING)	ISHMAEL (SINGING)
Ma tovu ohalekha Ya'akov, mishk'notekha Yisra'el.	Yalla tnam Rima, yalla yijeeha elnoum

Silence.

ISHMAEL
What will I do here? In Lebanon, Beirut?

MIRI
Try not to get kicked out.

ISHMAEL
And if they do kick me out?

MIRI
You go to Turkey then through Bulgaria, Serbia, Hungary, Slovakia, Poland into Germany.

ISHMAEL
That's a lot of borders.

MIRI
I will keep trying from my end-

ISHMAEL
When do you leave Beirut?

MIRI
In a couple of days. You can keep the hotel room for the week.

ISHMAEL
The world is so fucked up.

MIRI

Yeah. It is.

ISHMAEL

You know that place you are writing about? I can't get that place out of my mind.

MIRI

Cordoba?

ISHMAEL

You still blocked up?

MIRI

I don't know what's wrong with me.

ISHMAEL

You've written lots of books. I looked you up.

MIRI

You did?

ISHMAEL

So why is this one so hard?

MIRI

It feels like a world too far away. I have tried puppets, the museum-

ISHMAEL

You writing that book in English.

MIRI

It's the only language I have.

ISHMAEL

English is flat. No melody. It may be the most efficient language but it's the least poetic. Unless you fuck with it.

MIRI

You absolutely have to fuck with it.

ISHMAEL

Your verbs are confusing, your vowels are static My language is a game of self protection, a gated house where information is carefully chosen. You Westerners tell stories the same way you built railroads. In straight lines. My language is filled with twists and turns.

MIRI

In my country people assume when someone says something he means what he says.

ISHMAEL

That is why you get it all wrong in the press and mess up the world. How would you like some Arab journalist coming to America who doesn't speak English reporting back to the Arabs what he thinks he hears?

MIRI

Write it with me.

ISHMAEL

A book about peace in a language without poetry? We would kill each other in about forty minutes.

MIRI

A book about poetry in two languages of peace. We could love each other for about forty minutes.

> Miri takes out the same puppet she had been building in Iraq. It's finished now.

MIRI
This is the woman from an exhibit that used to be in the Islamic Wing of the museum. I'd stand in front of it for hours.

ISHMAEL
Who is she?

MIRI
I imagine she is a poet. She was in the exhibit with an man.

ISHMAEL
and him?

MIRI
I imagine he is a poet too. He was holding a paper and a feather pen.

ISHMAEL
They are Arab?

MIRI
I imagine she is Jewish and he is Arab.

ISHMAEL
Our tradition is full of great poets. I should know their names.

MIRI
Here's one: Abu al-Waleed Ahmad Ibn Zaydún (1003-1071) he was known as Zaydún of Cordoba.

ISHMAEL

A Proud Muslim laureate. Renowned for the power of his words. A prince at the top of his game. But I imagine he has The Doubt. Like you.

MIRI

Writer's Block?

ISHMAEL

I imagine a powerful man who has lost his voice. While this woman's poems pour out of her like honey.

MIRI (AS AVIVA PUPPET)

Come back here. Learn from us. How to make peace.

ISHMAEL

War will come.

MIRI (AS AVIVA PUPPET)

As it always does.

ISHMAEL

And we will have to take sides.

MIRI (AS AVIVA PUPPET)

Can you take Two sides?

ISHMAEL

Two sides.
You wanna cry for
Two sides
You buy
Guns for
Two sides

MIRI

They expire
Two sides

ISHMAEL

They are liars
Two sides

MIRI

They have kids
Two Sides

ISHMAEL

They <u>are</u> kids

MIRI AND ISHMAEL

Two Sides.

MIRI

You watch them bleeding
Two sides

ISHMAEL

Speeding Towards death

MIRI AND ISHMAEL

Two Sides.

ISHMAEL

They are leaning towards dark.

MIRI

No spark

ISHMAEL
Of hope

MIRI
Too cope

ISHMAEL
With dopes. Who sit in offices, point guns at maps: THERE, kill THAT,

MIRI
Spill that,

ISHMAEL
Grill that hill. With your Mohammed,

MIRI
Your Moses, your Christ.

ISHMAEL
Your Improvised Explosive Device.
MIRI
Far Wide

MIRI AND ISHMAEL
Two Sides.

A knock at the door. They look at each other. Another knock. Knocks continue.

MIRI
Room service?

ISHMAEL
Immigration.

MIRI

Housekeeping.

ISHMAEL

Isis.

MIRI

How would they know?

ISHMAEL

They know everything.

MIRI

Maybe it's a friend.

ISHMAEL

I don't have friends in Beirut.

MIRI

Neither do I.

ISHMAEL

Let's climb out the window. Is there a window?

MIRI

Let's just open the door.

ISHMAEL

Don't open the door!

MIRI

We'll have to open it eventually.

ISHMAEL

NO!

Pause.

MIRI
Then Let's go.

ISHMAEL
Go where?

MIRI
Cordoba.

ISHMAEL
I don't have a visa.

MIRI
How we go, you don't need one.

ISHMAEL
How do we go?

The knocking continues.

MIRI
The only road that's safe. Close your eyes.

He closes his eyes. She closes hers.

ISHMAEL
Imagine we are the only two people alive.

MIRI
Imagine we escape.

ISHMAEL
Escape Iraq. Escape Beirut. Escape / this –

                    MIRI
Escape this shit hole of a modern world.

                    ISHMAEL
Go back.

> They open their eyes and begin to transform the hotel room into an ancient tea room beneath the great Poetry Hall in Ancient Cordoba.

                    MIRI
Back to the Convivencia.

                    ISHMAEL
Back to our own history.

                    MIRI
Back past fascism,

                    ISHMAEL
Past genocide,

                    MIRI
Past airplanes and television,

                    ISHMAEL
One thousand years.

                    MIRI
One thousand years ago tonight.

> As lights shift the knocking becomes ancient music. Ishmael becomes ABU, circa 1015, in long robes with an ancient paper and a feather pen, trying to finish a poem. Miri now dressed

as Aviva, takes charge of the tearoom. Abu hides.
Aviva checks that she is alone. He watches her as
dives into her poem.

AVIVA

Wine party full swing.
Poets fling
Syllables, capturing rhymes
Poems about horses, poems about wine
Outsmarting the bold,
Out-braving the lofty.
Then CRASH
Sudden cold
Scattered Shattered
Shards of gold
Glass
The mood is dashed
The lively crowd
Stunned to silence
An old man points to the source of
Violence
One among them
Broken, unspoken
On the floor
As liquid billows
A dark red flood
Glazing golden pillows
His blood?
His Tears?
His Wine?
The Poet dazed,
Eyes ablaze
Trembling rhythm on
Twisted half smile fleeting
Beating

Up then down then up
The grip of some small hope still wet
On open lips
That cannot forget
The taste of pain
Forbidden woman
He left
Bleeding
In the rain.

>Abu steps out of the shadows. She sees him, she screams.

ABU

What was <u>that?</u>

>They stare at each other.

AVIVA

Sir?

ABU

You heard me.

AVIVA

It was nothing.

ABU

It was not nothing, It was indeed something. Who are you?

AVIVA

I thought the contest had begun. I thought everyone was downstairs.

ABU

Where is the tea servant?

AVIVA

I am the tea servant.

> She bows, quickly brings a bowl and water, kneels. He sits in front of her. She pours water over his hands.

ABU

Whose poem was that?

AVIVA

No poem, Sir.

ABU

ARE YOU DEFIANT?

AVIVA

No, Sir.

ABU

Who is the woman in the rain?

AVIVA

Sir?

ABU

In your poem.

AVIVA

You understand Hebrew?

ABU

You understand Arabic.

AVIVA
Of course I understand Arabic.

ABU
But you are not Muslim.

AVIVA
No.

ABU
And you are not Christian.

AVIVA
No, Sir.

ABU
Let me see your feet.

> She pulls up her long skirt revealing shoes of two different colors. He nods. She drops her hem.

ABU
I hate that law.

AVIVA
You are not alone.

ABU
Clown shoes to keep you in your place.

AVIVA
We rise above our shoes.
He chuckles.

ABU

I have seen you before.

AVIVA

No Sir, you have not.

ABU

You look familiar to me.

AVIVA

We all look the same.

ABU

Who all look the same? All Jews? All serving women? All poets?

AVIVA

I am not a poet.

ABU

I must say I have never heard a woman utter anything like that strange meter I just overheard. But let's not pretend it didn't happen.

She serves him tea.

ABU

Was that story in your poem from your own life?

AVIVA

Honey for your tea?

ABU

The love affair – the blood and the rain?

AVIVA
Would you like some bread?

ABU
Are you the forbidden woman?

AVIVA
Or cake?

ABU
Are you married?
Silence.

ABU
I ASKED YOU A QUESTION.

AVIVA
Yes.

ABU
Children?

AVIVA
A son.

ABU
Where are your husband and your son?

AVIVA
My son is at work. My husband is…

ABU
Where?

AVIVA
It's a long story.

ABU
Your husband abandoned you?

AVIVA
No! There was... trouble.

ABU
Did he kill one of your jealous lovers?

AVIVA
No.

ABU
Is he in prison?

AVIVA
No. He was sent away.

ABU
Why?

AVIVA
He was banished.

ABU
To wander in the desert like a Bedouin? But your people and mine are not pagan idol worshippers like Bedouins are we? We are civilized.

AVIVA
Yes, Sir.

ABU

And tolerant.

AVIVA

Yes, Sir. Except of course in our treatment of Bedouins.

ABU

What? Life in Cordoba is good for you Jews is it not?

AVIVA

Yes, Sir. Though we fear the enemies of peace that are gathering outside the city walls.

ABU

Even more reason why you Madame, should count your blessings.

She is silent.

ABU

Why was your husband sent away?

Silence.

ABU

WHO SENT HIM AWAY?

AVIVA

He fought with the Courtier Rabbi.

ABU

This sounds familiar.

AVIVA

No, Sir, it does not.

                        ABU
Where was he sent?

                        AVIVA
Back to the East. Al-Basrah.

                        ABU
I know this story.

                        AVIVA
No you do not.

                        ABU
Is your husband a poet?

            She busies herself with the tea.

                        ABU
SPEAK!

                        AVIVA
What will you be reading tonight?

                        ABU
You are avoiding my questions!

            She sees his paper. He covers it.

                        AVIVA
Is it one of your older poems or something new?

                        ABU
You know who I am?

AVIVA
Yes! Of course I know who you are!

ABU
Something new.

AVIVA
May I hear it?

ABU
Not ready. Hear it downstairs.

AVIVA
I won't be going downstairs.

ABU
The Jews don't allow their women into the hall?

AVIVA
I am allowed.

ABU
But you don't like it down there.

She doesn't answer.

ABU
I can guess the reason.

She is silent.

ABU
Arabic women read their poems in public why not Jewish women? Navisha bint Ahmad is famous for speaking a poem to a man who made her an unwelcome marriage proposal.

AVIVA

"I am a lioness, and will not sanction the use of my body for anyone – it will be me who calls consent, I would turn a deaf ear to most dogs, and how many a lion I have turned down!"

ABU

You know the poem. Now you know the man.

AVIVA

She wrote that about you?

ABU

She did.

AVIVA

You loved her?

ABU

She is a great writer.

AVIVA

She is my hero. She is the bravest most beautiful poet I have ever heard.
She embroiders her poems on her sleeves in gold thread. On the left arm: I am, by God, made for glory" On The right arm: I give my lover power over my cheek. Oh! Is that you she is speaking of? Are you the lover on her sleeve?

ABU

There are many lovers on Navisha's sleeve.

AVIVA

She is why I am working here – in hopes that she will stop for tea. She did once. With her magnificent hair and her golden sleeves. Could you introduce me to her?

ABU

No.

AVIVA

No?

ABU

She is not a very nice person.

AVIVA

You asked her to marry you.

ABU

She wanted my kisses, not to be my wife.

AVIVA

Do you have a wife?

ABU

I have three wives, but not a poet among them.

AVIVA

Navisha broke your heart.

He is silent.

AVIVA

What did you do?

ABU

I answered her. In a poem

AVIVA

Oh! Yes! I think I know it! Speak it! Please.

                    ABU
"She came unveiled in the night.
Each one of her glances
Could cause hearts to turn over.
But I clung to the divine precept
That condemns lust and reined in/
The capricious horses of my passion"

                    AVIVA
"The capricious horses of my passion
So that my instinct
Would not rebel against chastity.
And so I passed the night with her
Like a thirsty little camel
Whose muzzle keeps it from nursing."

                    ABU
You do know it.

                    AVIVA
It's poetic revenge.

                    ABU
All Poetry is inspired by fury.

                    AVIVA
Or hope. Or dream. Or story.

                    ABU
How would you know Mrs. Not-A-Poet?

                    AVIVA
I listen.

ABU

To whom?

AVIVA

To every person who is lucky enough to join the contest.

ABU

How? When you won't go into the hall.

> She goes to a loose tile in the floor and pulls it up, suddenly voices from downstairs fill the room. Arabic and Hebrew, a crowd talking at once.

AVIVA

It is a huge crowd tonight.

ABU

The Caliph is here.

AVIVA

It must be a special occasion.

ABU

He has come to hear my new poem. And some powerful men from outside Cordoba are with him.

AVIVA

You need to go down!

ABU

Not yet.

AVIVA

They sound like they are ready to begin the first battle.

ABU

Close that.

AVIVA

You will be late! If you are late you will not qualify for the Final Battle. If you come in after the third round they cannot accept a poem no matter who you / are.

ABU

CLOSE IT!

> She replaces the tile. Voices stop.

ABU

Your husband was here every week before his exile. That's where I have seen you, right? You are Bin Labrat's wife.

AVIVA

You are percipient, Sir.

ABU

You are recalcitrant, Woman. Am I right then? About your husband?

AVIVA

My husband, like you, is a famous poet.

ABU

A Jewish poet. Fame is relative.

AVIVA

He is renowned in our circles.

ABU
And was always watched carefully in ours.

AVIVA
You learn from him.

ABU
He stole from me.

AVIVA
How could he? He composes as a Jew.

ABU
With Arabic rhythms.

AVIVA
Hebrew letters.

ABU
Arabic vowels.

AVIVA
Jewish poems about Jewish issues.

ABU
Read in Muslim rooms in the Muslim world.

AVIVA
You don't like him.

ABU
He always took too much measure of himself.

AVIVA

Because he is a Jew?

ABU

That has nothing to do with it. I admire his work. He took a risk. He merged our traditions, our styles and rhythms. That is how he angered the Rabbis. Right? That's why he was sent away. Isn't it? He was an champion of assimilation.

AVIVA

Is. Is.

ABU

Your husband ... is ... a controversial instigator of poetic integration.

AVIVA

That is quite a distinction.

ABU

It's what our scholars say about him.

AVIVA

Then he is famous in your world as well.

ABU

And here you are Mrs. Wife-Of-A-Famous-Poet below the great contest hall serving tea. Seems unfair, does it not?

She pours tea. He watches her.

ABU

And do you also believe in collaboration between our peoples?

AVIVA

If there is equal power and equal voice.

####ABU
Are you a revolutionary?

####AVIVA
I will fight for justice.

####ABU
With uprising and bloodshed?

####AVIVA
Of course not.

####ABU
Then how?

####AVIVA
There is only one way to change the world.

####ABU
With Love?

####AVIVA
No. Poetry.

####ABU
"Will his love forget the gentle touch at midnight? The tiny boy, held tightly at her breast
He takes a golden ring with a yellow stone from his second finger/ and places it on her third..."

####AVIVA
"and places it on her third. They are almost broken, it will happen, now in moments. Disjoined sundered/ Would he stay there on that shore with his beloved, safely in Spain,"

ABU
"Would he stay there on that shore with his beloved, safely in Spain-"

AVIVA
"If the king would grant him rights of freedom?"

ABU
Your poem.

AVIVA
My husband's.

ABU
He reads it. You wrote it.

AVIVA
Nothing I claim.

ABU
But you must claim it, if it is yours.

AVIVA
It isn't.

ABU
AH. Yes! I see now. Obviously, it's not. The masculine elements in the poem are obvious. It was clearly written by a man. The symmetry, the form, the images of King and Country. No woman could be so bold, so steadily rhythmic, so comprehensive or analytical. No woman could have written such a poem.

AVIVA
That's ridiculous! Women are much more capable than men of writing such a poem! Rhythm is born in us! There is no man as

comprehensive as a woman. Analytical? We daily analyze ingredients for stew, medicines for fevers, the symptoms of a coming war, the best ways to hide the children. YOU COULDN'T WALK THREE STEPS WITHOUT US. WE WRITE THE POETRY OF YOUR LIVES!

He laughs.

AVIVA

You tricked me.

ABU

I have always found it interesting that Bin Labrat delivers such excellent poetry in the contest hall, he wins more often than not. But at wine parties, when he has to work spontaneously with a Saki's prompt he is rather/ weak-

AVIVA

You saw him at wine parties?

ABU

Your private style is much different from the one you use when you write for your husband. You are a poet, Madame.

AVIVA

I am a tea servant.

ABU

You may be a tea servant. But you are also the first Jewish poetess I have ever met.

AVIVA

Shhhh!

ABU

Tell me the truth now or I will shout downstairs to the Rabbis that a lascivious Jewess has been reaching up my robes. ARE YOU A POET? YES OR NO?

AVIVA

YES!

ABU

So why do you hide it? Ah. You are afraid.

AVIVA

Yes.

ABU

Of getting caught?

AVIVA

Yes.

ABU

Bad things would happen to you?

AVIVA

Our culture forbids women to be-

ABU

Creative?

AVIVA

Outspoken!

ABU

We poets are born outspoken. We are a strange breed.

AVIVA
Getting caught is not all I am afraid of.

ABU
What else?

AVIVA
I am afraid of not being good.

ABU
That is a ridiculous fear.

AVIVA
You have it.

ABU
What do you mean?

> She points to the paper in his hands.

AVIVA
Your paper. The harsh black stokes of ink – words have been crossed out and written over again and again. This is not the script of a confident man.

ABU
All Poets rewrite.

AVIVA
Of course. But not so violently.

ABU
It is only a passing moment of uncertainty.

AVIVA
When did you lose your trust?

ABU
It happened.

AVIVA
Suddenly?

ABU
One day I wrote a line and questioned it. The next day I doubted two lines. The third day I disputed the whole poem. I lost my flow.

AVIVA
This happened to my husband. You are scared of something.

ABU
I AM SCARED OF NOTHING!

Silence.

ABU
You don't understand the stakes. I have not had a win in seven weeks.

AVIVA
The Courtier Rabbi put similar pressures on my husband when he is not winning the contest.

ABU
It is not the same. My words are my only currency. If I don't come up with a masterpiece soon I am worthless to the court.

AVIVA
The Caliph wouldn't drive a sword through your heart for a bad poem?

ABU

I was by his side constantly until I started to lose. Fame is a potent allure but failure is just as mighty a revulsion. In the current climate I am vulnerable. The forces outside Cordoba are dangerous to me without the Caliph's favor.

AVIVA

Aren't you protected? Aren't you the grandson of a prince or something?

ABU

The Great Grandson of a King. But if I lose my place at court I have no protection. Tonight is my last chance and writing this damn poem is the hardest thing I have ever done.

AVIVA

Why is it so hard?

ABU

The judges want frivolity. Love poems. I want to write about God.

AVIVA

You are saying you cannot write because the fans call for language and you want to give them liturgy?

ABU

Not just liturgy, depth!

AVIV

I don't think the popular demand for light entertainment is your problem Sir.

ABU

WHAT DO YOU KNOW?

AVIVA

I can keep your secret. If you can keep mine. You are a celebrated poet and your people count on you for prolific fecundity. I understand that no one can know that you are stuck.

ABU

No one.

AVIVA

They say of you: With his speech he could tear the sea to tatters.

ABU

I should tear this paper to tatters.

AVIVA

Is that the poem you are reading tonight?

ABU

I am not sure I will read anything tonight.

AVIVA

Read it to me. I don't care how it sounds, just put the words into the room.

ABU

It's not-

AVIVA

Ready. I know. Read it anyway.

ABU

I do not read to a woman on command.

AVIVA

Don't you read to your wives?

ABU

They cannot comprehend my poems.

AVIVA

What about Navisha? I am sure she "can comprehend your poems".

ABU

We used to read our poems to each other. But that was long ago. The last poem she read was about me: "He is an insignificant fish. He is so in love with the rod in his own trousers, that is he would see a penis in a palm tree he would become instantly a bird."

   She bursts out laughing.

ABU

You admire her poetic skill?

AVIVA

The day I came upon Navisha, I whispered a poem to her as she drank her tea. I asked her to teach me, but then the contest started and she went downstairs and I never saw her again.

ABU

Tell me your poem.

AVIVA

No. It must have been abysmal. Otherwise she would have sent for me. She teaches poetry to women. But she never sent for me, so I know I am not good enough.

ABU
Navisha once spoke of a poem that was whispered to her by a serving woman.

AVIVA
No! What? Really?

ABU
Speak your poem.

AVIVA
If you read me yours, I will tell you mine.

ABU
I do not negotiate / with

AVIVA
With women, I know. But that is my offer.

ABU
Go ahead.

AVIVA
The sun abandons
Her eyes, suddenly
Like a sky of black birds fleeing northern winds
Barely visible through clouds that threaten rain.
Just as the gazelle leaps between trees,
Ephemeral
Untouchable
Her luminous heart
Escapes my arrows.
The instant I reach,
She vanishes.

The moment I look up,
No Sunlight.

>He is silent

AVIVA
What?

ABU
Nothing.

AVIVA
It's dreadful.

ABU
No.

AVIVA
What?

ABU
Nothing.

AVIVA
Then it's your turn.

ABU
To whom would I be reading?

AVIVA
Oh. Aviva.

ABU
Aviva... Would you like to know my name?

                    AVIVA
I know your name.

                    ABU
The name my brothers call me?

            She nods.

                    ABU
Abu.

                    AVIVA
Abu. Read.

                    ABU
"He stood still like a doe in winter…"

            He shakes his head.

                    AVIVA
Go on.

                    ABU
It's no good.

                    AVIVA
I don't care. Just read.

                    ABU
"One leg curled up wounded and useless…"

            Pause.

AVIVA

Abu. Keep going.

ABU

I cannot.

AVIVA

Let me.

    She reaches for it. He pulls it away. Reads:

ABU

"He stood still like a doe in winter
One leg curled up wounded and useless
He stood high above the craggy hill
One arm gone
He stood his black hair matted with battle
One face lifted
He stood bravely, a stone fountain lion…"

AVIVA

Is that it?

ABU

That's enough of it.

AVIVA

Who is He?

ABU

My brother. He deserves better than this terrible poem.

AVIVA

It's not terrible. We can work with it.

ABU

I do not allow a woman to tell me how to write!

AVIVA

Fine! Stay cemented in your verse-less prison.

Pause.

ABU

If my poems are no longer national treasures, the Caliph will send me out on the first horse when war comes. I do not know how brave a soldier I will be.

AVIVA

Will you kill me if they order you to?

ABU

May Allah never cause me to consider it.

AVIVA

May he protect you from that particular dilemma.
Pause.

AVIVA

Tell me about your brother.

ABU

I had five brothers. Now four.

AVIVA

I have four brothers. We played together like five boys in our garden.

My Heart is in the East

ABU

We had a garden with a huge fountain. A lion made of marble.

AVIVA

We had a fountain made of tiny rocks.

ABU

We had an orange tree from China.

AVIVA

We had a pear tree.

ABU

My mother baked pears with cardamom.

AVIVA

My mother baked rice with saffron. Lamb with dates / and Mint

ABU

And Mint.

AVIVA

As a baby I sucked on a rag soaked with mint and milk.

ABU

I had milk dripped into my mouth from a Ram's horn.

AVIVA

They washed my tongue with water every morning.

ABU

Me too, so my words would be pure.

AVIVA

Why "a doe in winter"?

ABU
Why did the poet kill the woman in the rain?

AVIVA
All love ends in death.

ABU
Not necessarily.

AVIVA
Love dies or people die.

ABU
She was bleeding.

AVIVA
Hearts bleed.

ABU
What was the odd meter you were using? Where is it from?

AVIVA
From my body.

ABU
What do you mean?

AVIVA
Comes into here.

Touches her ear.
It lodges here.

Touches her head.
This tells me if its right.

> Touches her stomach.

And if it's right, I speak it.

> Touches her mouth.

AVIVA
I guess a woman just told you how to write.

> Silence.

AVIVA
Can I touch your paper?

ABU
My paper?

AVIVA
I have never written on paper.

ABU
There are Jewish texts on paper.

AVIVA
The Rabbis have some. Ever since it came from China the holy men have coveted the stock.

ABU
But we make paper in Cordoba now.

AVIVA
It's too expensive.

> He offers it.

AVIVA
It is so light. Like the wing of a butterfly. Or a rose petal.

ABU
Do you write on parchment?

AVIVA
Parchment is to big to hide.

ABU
On what do you write?

> She taps her head.

ABU
You never pen anything?

AVIVA
I cannot risk it.

ABU
You must write them down for him. I've seen him reading.

AVIVA
I dictate, he writes.

ABU
If your husband is such a great poet why does his wife compose his poems?

AVIVA
It is my pleasure. And his gift. It is the only way I get my poems into the air.

ABU
So. It's a good marriage. Except that he used you and left you and you are serving tea eavesdropping on REAL poetry while hiding from your own.

AVIVA
You are jealous of/him _

ABU
Jealous? He is a piece of dirt.

AVIVA
HE IS A WONDERFUL / MAN!

ABU
What is so wonderful/ about him?

AVIVA
He is brilliant, an / innovator.

ABU
He steals your words. Why don't you tell the truth about/ that?

AVIVA
Why don't you tell the truth about your brother?

ABU
I don't want to talk about my brother.

AVIVA
I don't want to talk about my husband.

ABU
It's too bad you will never meet Navisha.

AVIVA

It's too bad you've lost your voice.

ABU

It's too bad no one will ever hear your poems now that your mouthpiece has been sent away!

AVIVA

YOU <u>ARE</u> AN INSIGNIFICANT FISH!

ABU

MY BROTHER IS DEAD!

> He storms out. She is about to pick up his pen but he rushes back in.

ABU

I can't go down there.

AVIVA

You have to go down there. Every minute you spend down here puts you at greater risk.

ABU

I know –

AVIVA

The contest has begun.

ABU

I KNOW!

AVIVA

At least let them see that you are here.

My Heart is in the East

ABU

My presence without a winning poem is as dangerous as my absence.

AVIVA

Then we should work on your poem.

ABU

I wish I could stop time.

AVIVA

Close your eyes.

He closes his eyes.

ABU

And now what?

AVIVA

Now imagine all there is in the entire world is poetry. Teach me the forms of Arab poems.

ABU

What?

AVIVA

Keep your eyes closed! Teach me how you use layers of rhythm to birth verse that is Earthy and True.

ABU

I doubt there is anything I can teach you about being Earthy and True, Aviva.

AVIVA

I know there is a Madih-

ABU

Madih, a eulogy, Hija, an insult poem, Ritha, an elegy, Ghazal, a love poem, Tardiyyah, hunt poetry, Hamasa, war poetry, Zajal, a shout.

AVIVA

I love this one of yours:
"The goblets were heavy
When they were brought to us
But filled with fine wine
They became so light
They were on the point of flying away"
What type of poem is that?

ABU

Khamriyyah, a wine poem.

AVIVA

Did you write it for a wine party?

ABU

Yes.

AVIVA

TELL ME ABOUT THE WINE PARTIES!

He opens his eyes and laughs.

ABU

You are very enthusiastic –

AVIVA

What are they like?

ABU

Did you never ask your husband?

AVIVA
He would never tell me anything about wine parties.

ABU
There are many things he never told you.

AVIVA
What do you mean?

ABU
Why are you so interested in wine parties?

AVIVA
Wine parties are the center of poetic life. And I am not allowed to go. Please!

ABU
The men sit in groups. Jews here. Muslims here. The Saki enters. He is a young man, a boy really, very attractive, manly but in his youth and dress almost feminine. He taunts the players into competition, pouring wine. Slyly challenging: " Is anyone here able to offer me a homonym?" The men scramble and push to be first.
He chooses one to begin and then twists the game again and again announcing "Now a poem on this sword" " That bowl" "The springtime" "A woman's leg" "A canal"-

AVIVA
A canal?

ABU
Anything that enters his pretty mischievous head. But there is never an evening without wine poems.

AVIVA
Let me try one. A Khamriyyah.

ABU

Fine. Here are the rules: First, I give you a spontaneous poem about wine and then you have to compose one of your own using the very same words but in your own manner.

AVIVA

Go!

Pause. He thinks. Then stands up and dives in.

ABU

Wine of smoke and mountain flower.
Thick dark rich red ripe grapes pressed to fluid
The mind, Gently drowning
Blood! Grapes! Sweetness!

He offers her the floor.

AVIVA

The grapes taste like delicious smoke and mountain flowers. Wine passes through eager lips along the river system of the blood until his mind in peace is drowned.

ABU

That's what you would write?

AVIVA

Yes. That's what I would write.

ABU

As him.

AVIVA

For him.

ABU
What would you write as you, for you?

AVIVA
Oh Red Ripe Grape
Oh Mountain Flower
Oh Lips
Oh Tunnel Oh smoke
Oh fire dancing
Up and down my rivered veins
Oh liquid, welcome
Drip drop drip
Whoosh
I am Going under
Oh let me drown some more!

ABU
You must have been drunk at least once to compose that.

AVIVA
I have only had sacred wine at special holidays.

ABU
The taste pleases you.

AVIVA
As it pleases God.

ABU
Does it please God to make your head light and your stomach warm?

AVIVA
It must.

ABU

I think men who say they are drinking to please God are either liars or fools.

AVIVA

Am I a liar or a fool?

ABU

You are certainly no fool.

AVIVA

Liar then?

ABU

Until you sing your poems in public you will always be covering the truth.

AVIVA

Covering the truth is different from lying.

ABU

How?

AVIVA

Lying is when you tell a story that you don't believe. For instance the holy men who pour wine down their throats and then write poems of abstinence.

ABU

We live in a world of paradox.

AVIVA

We live in two different worlds.

ABU

I learned Hebrew to read your Holy Bible.

AVIVA

You've read Torah?

ABU

I was fascinated.

AVIVA

By what?

ABU

By the fact that we are not so different. Your stories are much the same as ours. You have Jonah and the whale. We have Yunis and the whale.

AVIVA

I have read the Qu'ran.

ABU

You have?

AVIVA

It is a beautiful book.

ABU

It is.

AVIVA

We teach our children that reading the holy book is the greatest blessing in life. In our world Torah comes before everything.

ABU
We teach our children to read Arabic Poetry, then arithmetic and only after they have mastered those two do we teach them Qu'ran.

AVIVA
You have children?

ABU
Three.

AVIVA
One from each wife?

ABU
All from the first. The other two are quite young.

AVIVA
God help you.

ABU
God flood me like wine. I'd give/everything

AVIVA
Everything I own for that harp that lifts its song to God/ tonight

ABU
Tonight as the moon cuts a circle on his dark robe, written in / gold.

AVIVA
Who fathoms the mystery is shaken with/ love

ABU
There is no God but/ God.

AVIVA
God is one.

ABU
He forsakes his God for her dark hair.

AVIVA
She knows she is a lowly servant, he, a prince of poems.

ABU
Whenever you speak my hair stands up.

AVIVA
Your beauty cuts into my limbs.

ABU
My love is like

AVIVA
Sunlight at dawn

ABU
Fire at sundown

He moves closer.

ABU
I'd like to write a poem about you.

AVIVA
Me?

ABU
I'd write about the secret poet who pens the greatest poems under her husband's name.

> He comes close their lips almost touch, she pulls away.

AVIVA

"Is there anyone among you who can compose a homonym?"

ABU

On what, Madame Aviva?

> She looks around and picks up the teapot.

AVIVA

Tea!

ABU

She looked to the left
Where the teapot was left
With the hand on her right
She bowed to serve him the way that was right
And when up she rose
Her cheeks were blushed rose
And he knew her.

AVIVA

He "knew" her?

ABU

Rhyme! Pillow.

AVIVA

He lay his head on her feather... bed
In the fading light he slept like the dead
He dreamt of war in far off lands
As she used her strong and lovely hands
To smooth the danger from his brow

She wanted to calm him, and she didn't know how
His lips twitched, his eyes squeezed tight
Far from her arms, far from the light
In one hour she'd wake him. And the soldiers would take him
Out of her doors. And back to the wars.
So like the branch of a willow
She bowed her head to his... Pillow.

ABU

Took you long enough.

AVIVA

Free Verse! On Horses!

ABU

Four bristling thorny flanks steaming with magnificent fury-power, height, nose flaring feet kicking-

AVIVA

Mane flowing, gracefully leaping-

ABU

Kicking, stamping!

AVIVA

Leaping, flowing!

ABU

Leaping, stamping, kicking, flowing, power, fury. Horse.

AVIVA

Metaphor. On Stars!

ABU

There is no moon tonight, yet the heavens are bright with stars

AVIVA

Pin drops of fire

ABU

Her eyes are his starlight

AVIVA

His eyes are her warning.

ABU

Her lips are his windows. He opens her with his finger.

AVIVA

He thinks she is afraid. But he knows nothing.
She wants what she wants. She is Hungry. Heathen Glowing like an everlasting flame, It makes her an animal. Doe. Snake. Falcon.
She could take him in her beak Crush the juice out of his heart.

ABU

She could kiss him everywhere until he died of love.
Then swallow him whole. But she lets him live so he can drink her. It feels so strong. She'll submerge her ancient beginnings in his open mouth. No mortal this woman, she cares not for scruples or decorum. She is a musky lioness Drunk on blood and yes! She loves it.
She is the only female in the city of Cordoba like this.

AVIVA

He loses himself inside her. Then he locks her in a cave so know one will ever know the way she makes him tremble. He covers the entrance with huge stones until he can no longer smell her. He thinks she must be frightened. But he is blind.
Deep inside the cave she is still burning. She will always be blazing. She is the Hidden Fire of the world.

My Heart is in the East

He comes close to her.

ABU
We are so alike, you realize. You could be one of my wives.

AVIVA
No I could not.

ABU
You are an incredible woman.

AVIVA
I am a Jewish woman. Perhaps that is an exotic conquest for you. But you've got three women at home.

ABU
My wives don't understand me.

AVIVA
They understand you. But their job as wives does not require them to caress your arrogance. Can you imagine how many poems my husband could have published if he had three of me?

ABU
It is a holy shame that there is only one of you, Aviva.

AVIVA
Do not seduce me.

ABU
No. Between us it is different, it is-

AVIVA
What, "Love"?

ABU

No. Poetry.

AVIVA

Oh.

ABU

I have never had such a poetic exchange – not at the contest, not at a wine party.

AVIVA

I know.

ABU

I have called to God every night for help with my poem and he doesn't answer. But maybe he finally did. Maybe he sent me you.

AVIVA

He stood still like a doe in winter

ABU

Not a doe.

AVIVA

What then?

ABU

A proud young buck

AVIVA

A buck. He stood bravely/-.

ABU

Not stood, shook,

AVIVA
He vibrated-

ABU AND AVIVA
With life

He touches her.

AVIVA
My husband may be away, but he is still my husband.

ABU
He will never return.

AVIVA
You don't know that.

ABU
But I do, Aviva. I do.

AVIVA
What do you know?

ABU
I was jealous of your husband. Navisha was charmed by this prolific Jew. One night, at a wine party, she recited a poem a servant woman had whispered to her. He said the servant was his and so was the poem. That is why Navisha never sent for you. The poem is good. And, like all your other poems, it was stolen.

AVIVA
This can't be true.

ABU
It is true.

AVIVA

I convinced myself I was freeing the words from my heart and through his mouth they were finding their true home. What a fool. Everything is a lie.

ABU

Not everything. Think Aviva. What do you want?

AVIVA

Just once, to speak my poems at the contest.

ABU

Then you must do that.

AVIVA

It is impossible.

ABU

I have an idea.

AVIVA

What?

ABU

Take this off.

> He removes her head scarf.

ABU

I will cover your head in Muslim cloth and you will go down to the hall and recite your own poems.

> He puts his turban on her.

ABU
In Arabic. As a man. You will win every prize.

AVIVA
You want me to play for your side?

> He takes off her robe.

ABU
I want you to speak your poems in public.

AVIVA
They will kill me if they catch me.

ABU
If you trick them they will never suspect. Here.

> He takes off his robe. He puts his robe on her.
> They laugh. She walks.

ABU
No, no. Like this.

> He shows her how to saunter like a man.

AVIVA
Do I pass?

ABU
Keep your voice low and your eyes down.

> She deepens her voice.

AVIVA
GET ME MY TEA!

ABU
Yes, Sir.

He serves her tea.

ABU
The final battle is about to begin.

AVIVA
I want to meet Navisha.

ABU
You will meet her downstairs.

AVIVA
No. I will meet her here.

She puts her head scarf on him. He resists. She insists. He bows to her, becoming Navisha. In a woman's voice:

ABU
Come down, Sir. Let your excellent verses find their rightful place in the sun.

She pulls him to her and kisses him. She a man, he a woman. They dance, she leads. Aviva pulls away from him.

AVIVA
No!

ABU

No?

AVIVA

If I dress in your clothes and read my poems as a man, how will I free the voices of the women? You have inspired me to a fire for public speech I never knew I had. I am the wife of a poet, and the daughter of a poet, but you are right Abu, I am a poet. A mistress of verbs, Queen of syntax, Empress of metaphor. I take words out of my pocket – I throw them up, let them land on my shoulder. I can spit a sequence of vowels into a cup and it pours out like rich wine. Maybe I won't get to the contest. Maybe it will be my granddaughters or their granddaughters. But I promise you. My poems will someday be heard in a female voice. If I ever get the chance to speak my own poems in public it will as myself. A woman. A Jew.

> She takes his clothes off herself as he removes her clothes from himself. She puts her own clothes back on. He sits half dressed.

ABU

He was the youngest. He missed me terribly after I became famous. He followed me to wine parties, to every contest. He annoyed me. Cramped my style. He died three months ago, struck down in a street fight. He was defending my honor after I lost a contest. Every time I try to write, I see his face.

AVIVA

Write for him.

ABU

I try.

                            AVIVA
Read for him tonight.

                            ABU
This poem is not good enough.

                            AVIVA
Then make up a new one.

                            ABU
In your style?

                            AVIVA
On the spot.

                            ABU
Without paper.

                            AVIVA
You may not win.

                            ABU
I don't care.

                            AVIVA
Then go.

                            ABU
Will you come downstairs and listen?

                            AVIVA
No, Abu. I cannot skulk in the back of the contest hall. Or even above it anymore. But you must go downstairs and sing spontaneous songs of love. For both our peoples.

ABU

I have never done this. Get up at The Contest and…
Extemporize. Perhaps it is a bad / idea…

AVIVA

Abu! Arabic melodies have helped lift Hebrew from the grip of the holy men and into the mouths of the people: Justice, passion, homonyms, wine. We are the revolution. Together, in this time and place, we have called each other to beauty.

ABU

Tonight up far
Hangs one new star,
Shining like no other
Look! You see?
My brother.

AVIVA

Di assedah gamela gedan.

ABU

Toda.

AVIVA

Shukran.

ABU

Shalom.

AVIVA

Ma sa-lama.

>He hands her his paper and exits. Aviva picks up his pen. She writes for the first time on paper.

Knocking. Lights shift. Aviva becomes Miri, still writing. Abu returns as Ishmael. They are back in the hotel room in Beirut.

ISHMAEL

Fuck.

MIRI (WRITING)

Wine party full swing.

ISHMAEL

What the fuck / was –

MIRI (WRITING)

Poets fling,

ISHMAEL

Miri?

MIRI (WRITING)

Homonyms? Capturing rhymes?

ISHMAEL

Miri!

MIRI (WRITING)

Poems about horses! Poems about wine-

ISHMAEL

What are you doing?

MIRI

Finishing what I started.

ISHMAEL
MIRI! Look at me!

MIRI (WRITING)
I have to write it down. I don't want to forget anything.

ISHMAEL
You are fierce, Miri. Look at you writing a storm.

MIRI
Writing a storm.

ISHMAEL
What do we do now?

MIRI
We need a plan.

ISHMAEL
A plan?

MIRI
A pledge.

ISHMAEL
A pledge to what?

MIRI
To watch out for each other.

ISHMAEL
A promise?

MIRI
A promise to remember.

ISHMAEL/MIRI

Cordoba.

MIRI

To be brave.

ISHMAEL

Women are braver than men, I think. You are better at carrying…

MIRI

Carrying what?

ISHMAEL

The whole world.

> The knocking gets louder. He walks towards the knocking.

MIRI

What are you doing?

ISHMAEL

Finishing what I started.

> He goes to the door knocks back to the knocking. His rhythm becomes a drum beat. He beats on everything in the room.

ISHMAEL

Come on ICE MAN. I ain't afraid Not gonna Shit myself, won't get crazed.
Lock me up with a little black bug – or shoot me dead, my grave's been dug

> Miri joins the beat and together they drum over the knocking.

ISHMAEL

But you can't take the bump of me,
Can't nab the thump, the high jump,
The thrill of my timing, can't steal my rhyming.
Can't filch my stomp, can't thieve my romp,
My pomp and circumstance. My dance.
You can capture my nation, cause my frustration, force my stagnation, my starvation. But you can't kill my imagination.
It's too fleet.
You can cut off my feet,
But can't never not never Take my BEAT.

> The knocking stops. They turn to look at each other.

MIRI
The final song of our strange love story?

ISHMAEL
Without solution, without glory?

MIRI
Deep at sea in a school of sharks,

ISHMAEL
Instead of answers, more question marks.

MIRI
Man versus woman, Arab versus Jew
East versus West, Red versus Blue.

ISHMAEL
There are some who fight to see rays of light

MIRI
In this dark cold world where it's mostly night.

ISHMAEL
A distant glint in their upturned eyes,
Look! A slight bright gash in the shadowed skies.

MIRI
And through the breach from either side
Fly two flocks of birds with wings spread wide.

ISHMAEL
One mob predator, one swarm prey
There will be blood by end of day.

ISHMAEL AND MIRI
OR

MIRI
Perhaps the field on which these birds alight

ISHMAEL
Won't be the scene of a gory fight.

MIRI
Perhaps the Gods that favor geese

ISHMAEL
Will prevail on these birds for peace.

MIRI
Perhaps the hound won't bite the fox

ISHMAEL
And we'll make friends with paradox.

MIRI
Perhaps Ishmael we have grown wise

ISHMAEL
Perhaps we've learned to take both sides.

ISHMAEL AND MIRI
Perhaps.

> A paper airplane flies in. They watch it. Just it before lands, blackout. As the lights slowly fade up on an empty stage we hear the recorded voices of 3 Men and 3 Women of different ages, cultures and ethnicities as in the very beginning.

WOMAN ONE
It's <u>our</u> decision,

MAN ONE
Our choice,

WOMAN TWO
Dear friends.

MAN TWO
How will this story reach its end?

WOMEN
Will one of us triumph over the body of the other?

MEN
Will she be my killer, will she be my lover?

JESSICA LITWAK

WOMAN THREE
Will our greed drown out the dying earth?

MAN THRE
Will we open our eyes, find hope, give birth?

WOMEN
Will he colonize me, or bow his head?

MEN
This time next year – alive or dead?

WOMAN ONE
Not much left to contemplate

MAN ONE
The time has come to decide our fate

WOMAN TWO
We must act fast

MAN TWO
To choose which track

WOMAN THREE
And solve the riddle

MAN THREE
Before the lights go black.

WOMEN
In our vast lost choir what deeds ring through?

MEN

And faced with war,

WOMEN	MEN
What will WE do?	What will WE do?

Music. End of Play.

www.ingramcontent.com/pod-product-compliance
Lightning Source LLC
Chambersburg PA
CBHW051655040426
42446CB00009B/1141